Date: 3/10/14

First Facts

A Thanksgiving DRAWING Feast!

by Jennifer M. Besel

illustrated by Lucy Makuc

CAPSTONE PRESS
a capstone imprint

First Facts are published by Capstone Press,
1710 Roe Crest Drive, North Mankato, Minnesota 56003
www.capstonepub.com

Library of Congress Cataloging-in-Publication Data
Besel, Jennifer M.
A Thanksgiving drawing feast! / by Jennifer M. Besel ; illustrated by Lucy Makuc.
pages cm.—(First facts. Holiday sketchbook)
Includes bibliographical references and index.
Summary: "Step-by-step instructions and sketches show how to draw common Thanksgiving
and autumn images and symbols"—Provided by publisher.
ISBN 978-1-4765-3093-2 (library binding)
ISBN 978-1-4765-3424-4 (ebook pdf)
ISBN 978-1-4765-3448-0 (pbk.)
1. Thanksgiving Day in art—Juvenile literature. 2. Drawing—Technique—Juvenile literature.
3. Autumn in art—Juvenile literature. I. Makuc, Lucy. II. Title.
NC825.T48B47 2014
743'.893942649—dc23   2013005602

Editorial Credits
Juliette Peters, designer; Kathy McColley, production specialist

Photo Credits
Capstone Studio: Karon Dubke, 5 (photos); Shutterstock: Markovka, design element

Printed in the United States of America in North Mankato, Minnesota.
032013   007223CGF13

Table of Contents

Filling up on Art

Football and pumpkins
and turkey to chew.
Thanksgiving is fun,
and learning to draw is too!

Feast your eyes on the fun, simple projects in this book. Just follow these tips and the easy steps on each page. You'll be drawing the sights of Thanksgiving in no time.

TIP 1 **Draw lightly.** You'll need to erase some lines as you go, so draw them light.

TIP 2 **Add details.** Give your drawings an extra helping of awesomeness with fun details, such as blowing leaves or silly signs.

TIP 3 **Color your drawings.** Color can make a good drawing even better!

You won't need pans to cook up these
drawings. But you will need some supplies.

drawing paper

pencil

eraser

colored pencils
or markers

pencil sharpener

Sharpen your pencils, and get ready to draw the
sights of Thanksgiving. **It'll be a fantastic drawing feast!**

Pumpkin Patch

Pumpkins are the perfect Thanksgiving decoration. Their orange color matches the falling leaves. And they make excellent pies!

Final

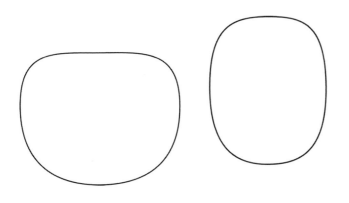

 Draw one short, fat oval. Draw one tall oval next to the first one.

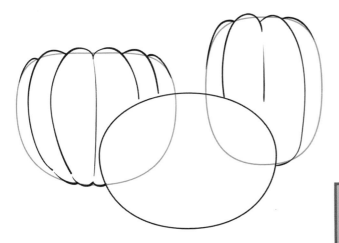

 Draw another oval in front of the first two. Add detail lines to the pumpkins in back.

Don't Forget!
Erase lines that go under something else. For example, erase the lines that go through the front pumpkin in step 2.

 Draw stems on all three pumpkins. Add detail lines to the one in front. Draw leaves blowing around the pumpkins. Add more leaves around the bottom.

Tip Your Hat

You could draw and cut out Pilgrim hats to decorate the table. Just remember to take off your hat before you eat!

Final

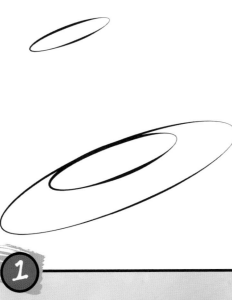

1

Draw a large circle. Then draw
a smaller circle inside the first.
Draw an even smaller circle way
above the first two.

2

Draw a line from the left edge of the
small circle to the edge of the inside
circle below. Repeat on the right side.
Add a curved line inside the hat.
Then add a detail line around the brim.

3

Draw a square in the middle
of the hat band. Draw a smaller
square inside the first to make
a buckle.

4

Add detail lines to the buckle
to make it look 3-D.

Piece of Pie

It's not Thanksgiving without pumpkin pie.
Top your drawing off with a swirl of whipped
cream. It will be the sweetest drawing ever!

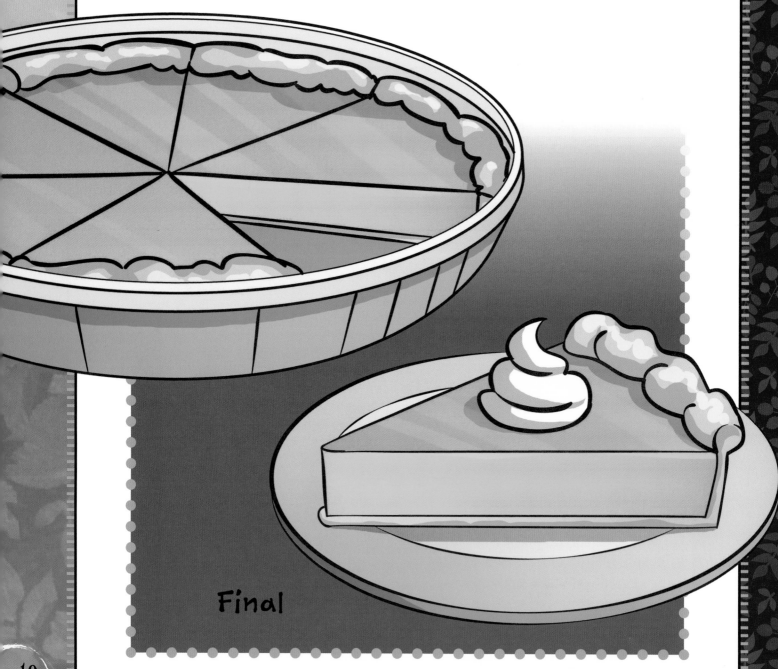

Final

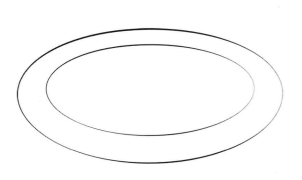

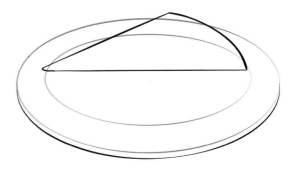

1

Draw one large circle. Then draw a smaller circle inside the first one.

2

Draw a triangle on the plate. Add a half circle below the large circle to make the plate look 3-D.

3

Draw a scalloped line on the right side of the pie. Add detail lines below it to make the pie look thick. Use scalloped lines to put a bit of whipped cream on top.

4

Add another scalloped line on the right side of the pie to finish the crust. Add detail lines to the whipped cream to make it swirl.

Thanksgiving Kicks

Remember the American Indians at the first Thanksgiving with this project. Afterward kick off your shoes, and take a Thanksgiving nap.

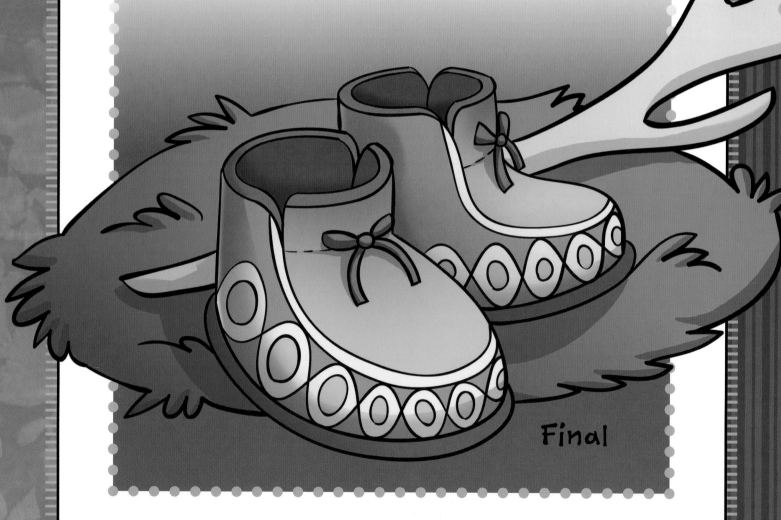

Final

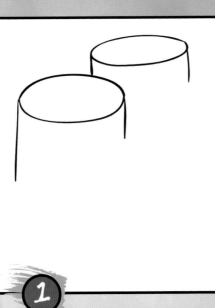

1

Draw a small circle. Draw straight lines down from each side. Repeat to start a second shoe behind the first.

2

Draw small circles inside the first circles. Use curved lines to draw the main part of each shoe.

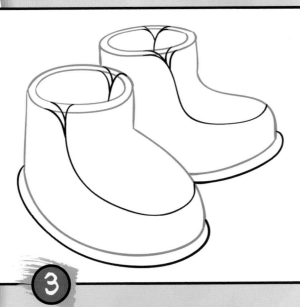

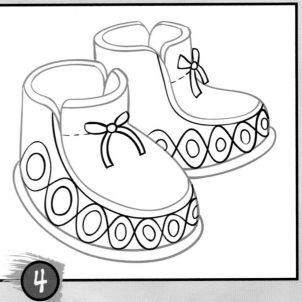

3

Draw curved lines inside each shoe to make the top. Add detail lines around the bottoms as soles.

4

Draw stitch marks and bows on the tops of each shoe. Add a detail line around the line that made the top. Then add circle decorations around the bottom of each shoe.

Mayflower

Celebrate the Pilgrims' trip across the ocean. Add a few waves to sail this famous ship right onto your refrigerator.

Final

1

Draw a small rectangle. Then draw a longer rectangle to the right of the first one. Add three long poles to the top.

2

Use straight lines to draw the bottom of the boat.

3

Draw triangle flags at the tops of the middle and right poles. Draw two "L" shapes below each flag. Add a diagonal line on the left pole.

4

Use curved lines to turn the "L" shapes into sails. Finish the sail on the left pole with curved lines. Finally add detail lines to the back and front of the ship.

15

Gobble!

Turkeys are the stars of Thanksgiving. But they wish people would gobble up chicken instead.

EAT CHICKEN

Final

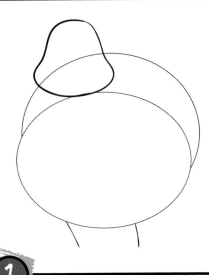

1

Draw an oval. Then draw half an oval above the first one. Add a bell shape for a head. Then add two short lines to start the legs.

2

Use scalloped lines to draw wings on the right and left sides. Draw the start of the beak on the head. Below the beak add the wiggly flap of skin called a wattle.

3

Use curved and straight lines to turn the half oval into tail feathers. Add details to the beak. Then draw two toes on each foot, and add leg feathers.

4

Give your turkey eyes, and finish its beak. Add details to the tail feathers. Finally, draw two more toes on each foot, and add detail lines.

Cornucopia

In stories the cornucopia has an endless supply of food. Draw your own magical horn. You can't eat it, but you can draw as much food as you want!

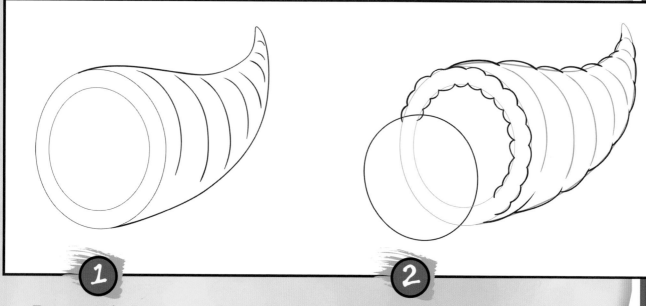

1

Draw a circle. Draw a smaller circle inside the first. Use curved lines to draw a horn shape off the first circle. Add detail lines to the horn.

2

Draw a circle in front of the horn. Use scalloped lines to add details to the horn's front and sides.

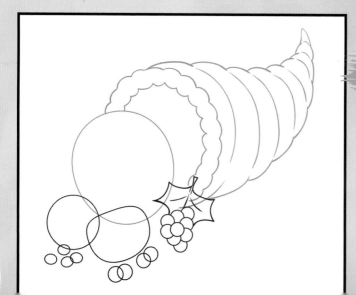

3

Add circles of different sizes around the front of the horn. Also draw a leaf shape.

4 Add stems to the circles to make them look like pieces of fruit. Add leaf shapes to fill in the area inside the horn and around the fruit.

5 Add detail lines to the fruit and leaves to make your cornucopia overflow.

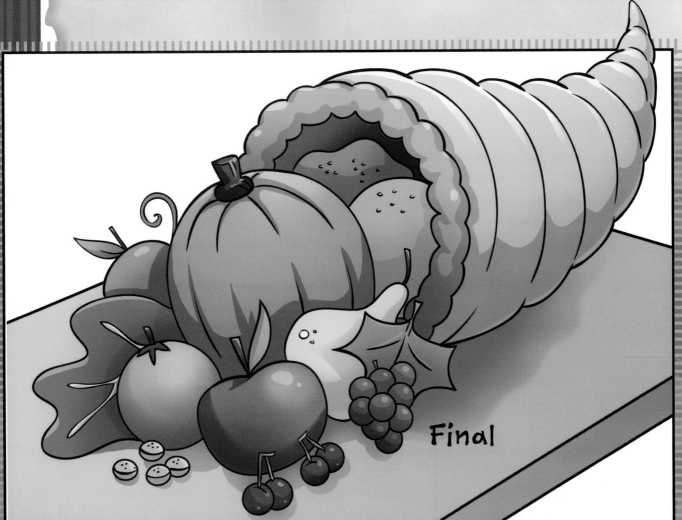

Final

Blown Away

Thanksgiving time brings cool winds and falling leaves. Draw this project, and you'll blow away your friends and family.

1 Draw a long rectangle to start the body. Add a circle on top. Below the body draw bent rectangles to start legs.

2 Use scalloped lines to add hair and an ear to the character. Use curved lines to draw a shirt and the start of a scarf.

3 Draw more hair and an ear on the other side. Add curved lines to the scarf. Draw a sleeve to the right side and mitten hands to both arms. Draw small ovals for shoes.

4 Add detail lines to the hair, ears, scarf, and shirt. Draw ovals for eyes. Then give the character a nose, mouth, and eyebrow.

5 Add more detail lines to the shirt, pants, and scarf. Draw a small oval inside each eye for pupils. Finish by drawing curly wind lines.

Final

Touchdown

Race to the end zone with this project. Your awesome drawing will definitely score you some points.

1 Draw a rounded rectangle for a body. Add a circle on top. Draw a curved line inside the circle head to start the hair. Add a small rectangle arm on the side of the body. Use curved lines to start a leg.

2 Draw scalloped lines for hair around the inner hairline. Add ears, a nose, and the start of the mouth. Use curved lines to add a second arm and another leg.

3 Use curved lines to draw pony tails on both sides of the head. Draw eyes, and add detail to the mouth, ears, and pants. Add basic hand shapes to the arms. Then draw "L" shapes to start the shoes.

4

Give the character eyebrows. Draw a football shape over the bent arm. Add fingers to the hand on the other arm. Give the player a number on her shirt. Then finish the shoes.

5

Add detail lines to the character's hair and football.

Final

Read More

Besel, Jennifer M. *A Halloween Drawing Spooktacular!* Holiday Sketchbook. North Mankato, Minn.: Capstone Press, 2014.

Court, Rob. *How to Draw Thanksgiving Things*. Doodle Books. Mankato, Minn.: Child's World, 2008.

Rissman, Rebecca. *Thanksgiving.* Holidays and Festivals. Chicago: Heinemann Library, 2011.

Internet Sites

FactHound offers a safe, fun way to find Internet sites related to this book. All of the sites on FactHound have been researched by our staff.

Here's all you do:

Visit *www.facthound.com*

Type in this code: 9781476530932

Super-cool stuff! Check out projects, games and lots more at
www.capstonekids.com